THE
P.E.A.R.L.S. Movement
MILLENNIALS ON THE MOVE

PEARLS for A Mindset Reset
Reset Your Mind for Success!

*"The 10 Commandment Pearls to
help you reach your dream!"*

Library of Congress 2020

Copy write © 2020 by Dr. Rael Bowie

Lulu PUBLICATIONS

ISBN # 978-1-67801-285-4

PEARLS of A Mindset Rest – Reset Your Mind for Success

Author: Dr. Rae Bowie

This book is gifted to:

_____

From: _____

You are an awesome Millennial

For the Jones Family

PEARLS for A Mindset Reset
Reset Your Mind for Success!

"The 10 Commandment Pearls to help you reach your dream!"

Natural pearls form when an irritant - usually a parasite works its way into an oyster, mussel, or clam. As a defense mechanism, a fluid is used to coat the irritant or invader. Layer upon layer of this coating, called 'nacre', is deposited until a lustrous pearl is formed.

CONTENTS

✸

Dear Millennial,

This is your season for success. Push the reset button and restart your motivation to win!

It doesn't matter what has happened yesterday or last year, as long as you have breath in your body with a sound mind you can, and you will move to the next level of your life.

You are the future generation that will change this world. You have been blessed to have the wisdom of your grandparents and the passion from your parents all of whom have given you the courage to be an amazing free-thinking generation.

Now, let's go make this paper!

Don't Shoot the Messenger!

❧

Millennials don't allow yourself to be tricked into thinking that the majority of the world is against you. We are not.

To be perfectly honest with you, you are a combination of the shifting of the universe at the time you were conceived in your mother's womb, and the product of your environment as you were raised.

Your mindset and the way you see things is not a mistake or an accident. People are often confused as to how or why you think and act the way you do; it is because your birth was an answer to a much greater cause.

Believe it or not the millennials are the answer to a call that went out into the universe to correct a world that has become increasingly, greedy, cynical, racist, mean spirited and lifeless.

Millennials were born from a generation of people that were passionate and creative yet indoctrinated, and damaged. Because of this what parents from that generation, me included, gave our millennial children was only a portion of what our parents gave us. In some instances, the complete opposite of what our parents gave us. In turn gave our millennial children more understanding, more freedoms, and more material things which resulted in and more choices for them which resulted in poor choices for both us, and our millennial children.

Millennials are more about the core of who people are rather than the race of people. They are more about living and let live than any other generation.

Don't Hate the Player, Hate the Game...Wait,

Don't Hate the Game, Learn How to Play to Win!
❧

Millennial, it is no secret that "Life" has been identified as a game. It has been compared to a game of chess, a game of baseball and a game of cards. Relationships between men and woman have been compared to the cat and mouse game of chase, or the dog and cat game of chase. Life in general has been identified as a set of rules spoken and unspoken; those who pay attention to the details, listen to what is not being said, those that read between the lines and the ones that never give up are the ones that win. Somehow the unspoken rules "trip" up most people, and these individuals tend to call "foul" play. They find themselves always on the losing end. Because of this, they become bitter and they hate the "Players" and the "Game".

Millennial, the best revenge is succeeding and becoming that which they said you couldn't. The best way to do that is right here, right now, in the pages of this book.

The 10 Commandment Pearls

❧

Commandment Pearl 1

❧

"I Shall Set the Intentions for My Day"

Most of us will agree that making a plan for your day is a great way to start your day. We have been taught that failing to make a plan is a sure way that we will fail. This is our old way of thinking. It is time for a mindset reset.

Stop making a plan for your day and a plan for your life, instead set your intentions for your day and for your life.

Setting your intentions for your day is more than writing out a "To-do list" of tasks that you need to complete.

Setting your intentions for your day is more about telling the universe what your heart and mind intend to accomplish through the manifestation of a course of events that your body intends to complete.

When setting your intentions for your day you must be clear as to what you intend to accomplish. Most of us are use to just going through our day and being reactive to how the day has played out. This way of living has caused many of us to miss deadlines, be distract by family and friends and waist time. We then end up putting off what you could have done today for tomorrow.

When you set your intentions for the day, with a clear and concise course of action, the universe will respond within your flow and whatever you need to get your intentions done will cross your path. It is up to you to pay attention to what you need.

The same rule applies to your life. We don't live out our lives all in one day. Therefore, each day is a representation of our intentions for our life.

When you are writing your goals to get to your dreams, write them with the "intention" of completing them. Literally write them out like this:

"I intend to" ... or "My intentions are" ...

Commandment Pearl 2

❧

"I Shall Listen to Motivational Material Daily"

Ask yourself, do you want to be just "great" or do you want to be "exceptional"?

We spend many hours on our cell phones, on the internet and watching television shows. While these things may have a place for entertainment in our lives, if you plan on achieving your dreams, the amount of time that you spend doing these activities must drastically change.

The difference between great people and exceptional people in my opinion is a thin line. But this thin line makes all the difference in the world. For some people this thin line may seem like an ocean that is impossible to cross.

Both, the "Great" and the "Exceptional" person have vision, great work ethics, and both are committed. However, "Great" people do the work to achieve the goal. They take great notes and pay close attention. Then they apply what they have learned. When they have achieved their goals, they stop doing the basic work. The "Great" person starts to enjoy the fruit of their labor.

The "Exceptional" person is the one that continuously feeds their minds motivational material that keeps them connected to their higher consciousness. The higher consciousness person is always open to receive new opportunities, and new insight.

We live in a world that doesn't care if we are inspired or encouraged. Most people are just happy to make ends meet. When you constantly feed your mind with motivational material your perspective about live will begin to change. If you want something that you have never had, you must be willing to become a person you have never been.

To become a successful person, you must become a "reader" of books, a listener of motivational audio and video.

Doing the tasks to complete your dreams is more than half the work. Success is not only completing the tasks, but it is a mindset. To stay in a successful mindset, you must continue to find your mind successful stories of accomplishments.

Commandment Pearl 3

❧

"I Shall remove toxic people out of my life"

Toxic people breed toxic situations that kill spirits and dreams. You are ready to take your life to the next level moving towards your dreams, you must act now taking steps to get toxic people out of your life. You must act now to take steps to remove yourself from toxic situations in your life. This may be a hard thing to do, but it is necessary.

The toxic people may be people that we really love. These may be the people that we are actually working so hard to become successful for.

It is not your job to fix your family or your friends. You cannot change them. You have enough on your plate trying to change yourself. If they are toxic to your success, you have a choice to allow them to infect your life with their toxicity or you can remove yourself from their environment.

Some people you will need to completely cut them off, forget you ever knew them. Some people you can remove them from your immediate environment, and you love them from a distance.

Don't kid yourself into thinking that you can keep toxic people in your space and still reach your dreams, you can't.

Commandment Pearl 4

❦

"I shall find a mentor"

On this journey to success it is important to have a mentor or a life coach that can help you stay the course and be accountable for your activities.

Whatever dream you have of making money and becoming successful chances are that there are other people out there in the world that have done the exact same thing that you want to do. If not the exact same thing, something similar.

Do your research and reach out to them. If you are not able to find someone in the field that you want to go into, then find someone that may know someone that has a mindset of success and ask them to mentor you.

Finding a mentor may not be an easy task. However, you must put yourself in places where successful people go to feed their minds and spirits. Go to seminars, workshops, and conferences. When your mind sends out the frequency of help, the universe will answer with your mentor.

Commandment Pearl 5

❧

"I Shall Be Specific When I Speak"

When you ask most people what it is that they want out of life, they can't tell you what they want. But they can tell you what they don't want. We concentrate more on what we don't want because we are not clear as to what we really want.

The bad thing about concentrating more on what we don't want is we are sending this signal out to the universe. We send out frequencies of what's on our minds the most, and the Universe response with a mirror reflection of what we are sending out. In essence we get more of what we don't want, because that is what we are thinking on the most. Instead of what we want.

You can think one thing and speak something completely different. Perhaps you are conflicted in your feelings about a situation. When you speak something different than what you are thinking you are communicating to the universe that you are confused. Therefore, the universe responds with more situations that will cause you to be confused or conflicted.

Make it a habit to start speaking in very specific details. Not using too many words or rambling but be précises and deliberate with your words. Don't speak unless you are sure of what you are going to say and why you are going to say it.

Often times people speak and have no clue as to why they said what they said. Sometimes we have to back pedal when we say things that weren't well thought out.

Know your audience, and be specific and deliberate when speaking, so that no one is left wondering what you meant. Of course, there will be times when people will take what you said and interpret it the way they received it and it was not how you intended. But with practice you will learn how to speak specific and deliberate and the universe will do the rest for you.

Commandment Pearl 6

※

"I Shall Not Deny but Defy"

In our quest for success we are leaning several important things. We are learning the importance of being positive and speaking specific and deliberate, removing toxic people and things out of our lives. Also, we should transmit the energy to the universe that which we want the universe to transmit back to us.

In all of that we must also know that bad things will happen to us. Just because we are ready for success and doing everything that we know to do doesn't mean that "life" isn't going to throw a curve ball at us. Some of us are already in situations that are so bad that we have one eye open and one closed. We have closed our one eye to the bad things and looking at the good things with the one eye opened.

The reality is we cannot deny the bad. On this journey we must recognize the bad and the good. It is not about bad things happening its about how you get through the bad things. It's also about what you allow the bad things to do to you and what you take from the bad things that happen.

Don't deny the situation defy it. Beat it! You cannot conquer a battle that you are not willing to confront. In order to confront it you must recognize its existence. Lying and hiding about it will only keep you from being free to pursue your dreams.

Commandment Pearl 7

❧

"I Shall be Early"

There is a saying that goes like this; "The early bird gets the worm". There is another one that says, "If you are on time you are late". I know that you have heard at least one of those sayings. Being early sets you apart from the crowd.

Being early says: "I'm ready", "I'm interested", "I'm reliable", "I'm Couscous", and "I am respectful of other people's time".

When you arrive early to your appointments something happens to the way you conduct your day. When you set your intentions for the day to be early you are setting yourself up to complete all your intentions for the day.

This change of mindset can really change your atmosphere. It will also change the way people deal with you. Being early allows you to get relaxed, get your mind prepared, and scope out your environment.

Being a person that arrives early sets an impression in people's mind about you that you are the person that takes care of business and you are serious about your mission. People respect other people that respect time.

Commandment Pearl 8

છ

*"I Shall Work on
My Communication Skills"*

People can assume what you know by looking at you. But it isn't until you open your mouth to speak that confirms it.

Effective communication skills are essential to success in achieving any goals that we have. In the 21st Century we have moved away from in person face to face communication and texting, internet chat rooms, instant messenger, emails and video chats are the acceptable way to communicate.

Whichever way you find is the best way for you to communicate, you still need to make sure that you are communicating effectively.

It is not necessary for a person to get their college degree to learn how to effectively communicate. There are far too many books, podcasts, and videos on the subject for one not to learn how to effectively master the art of communication.

One of the most important things in communication is vocabulary. To expand your vocabulary, you should look in the dictionary or thesaurus and learn a new word every week. Study the word by writing it down and use it in your conversations throughout the week. Before you know it, you will have expanded your vocabulary.

Active listening, and objective listening is also important for effectively communicating. When you are actively listening, you are able to repeat back to the person you are talking to what you heard them saying before you actually give your opinion or answer. Doing this ensures that both you and the other person is on the same page.

Listening objectively, simply means that you are only going on the facts of the situation and not your personal feelings about it the situation.

When writing any kind of communication, you must be aware of your audience, especially when selecting phrases, emojis and acronyms. This form of communication is the most misinterpreted way of communication. Because your words are subject to the person's attitude who is reading what you wrote at that time.

Learn the art of communication, this is a necessary tool to reach your dreams.

Commandment Pearl 9

❧

"I Shall Upgrade My Relationships"

Chickens fly, but they don't fly high. Eagles soar high above the clouds. "Birds of a feather flock together" is a saying that my mother used to say to me often when I was growing up. She said this to me because she wanted me to take a look at who my friends were. She wanted me to see that in nature all species run with their own kind. In essence she was asking me, "are you doing what your friends are doing?" More importantly she wanted to know if

I wanted to be "known" for what my friends are "known" for.

If you are the smartest person in your crowd you need a new crowd. Success is not for everyone, and not everyone wants to be successful.

Many people are fine just being mediocre. You are not mediocre. We are defined by the company that we keep. It may seem unfair, but it is a fact. You cannot change people that want to be mediocre and are ok with living a menial existence.

Your mission is to surround yourself with people that are doing the same thing that you want to do. This is the way in. When you make up in your mind that you are going to accomplish your dreams no matter what, you will automatically be drawn to people that are living the life that you want.

One of my mentors, Less Brown would say, only deal with quality people. Stop wasting your time with people that want to party all the time, are irresponsible and have no desire to excel or move from the status that they are in now.

To get something you have never had, you have to become someone you have never been. You can't do that hanging out with your hommies, or your girlfriends that has no vision and cannot see past their current situation.

Commandment Pearl 10

꙯

*"I Shall Face the Fear That is
Keeping Me from Succeeding"*

Push the reset button on your brain. Don't allow fear to keep you from what you want. Fear has been said to be "false evidence appearing real". Fear only has as much power as you give it.

Each person's situation is different; therefore, you may have a legitimate reason to be afraid. However, you have to face that fear head on if you ever intend on being free from it. If you face it head on you can analyze the situation and break it down to understand why you are afraid. Sometimes the situation itself is scarier than the details within the situation.

By you allowing fear to dictate your moves you are putting locks and chains on your dreams. Unlock yourself from fear and move about the world free.

This book and the entire P.E.A.R.L.S. series
are Inspired by these great individuals:

> *Less Brown*
>
> *Oprah Winfrey*
>
> *Earl Nightingale*
>
> *Napoleon Hill*
>
> *Andrew Carnegie*
>
> *Wayne Dyer*
>
> *Zig Ziglar*
>
> *Sadhguru*
>
> *Deepak Chopra*

The Millennials on the Move PEARLS
series by
Dr. Rae Bowie:

The P.E.A.R.L.S. Movement

PEARLS of A Boss *"Bitch"*

PEARLS of A Boss *"Zaddy"*

PEARLS for MY LGBTQ+ Friends

PEARLS for Obtaining Financial Success

www.ingramcontent.com/pod-product-compliance
Lightning Source LLC
Chambersburg PA
CBHW060201070426
42447CB00033B/2251